This book is dedicated to
everyone who is in recovery.

Happiness Is...

Adventures in
self discovery

Being true to yourself

Creating a life you love

Disposition not
circumstance

Enjoying what you have

Finding balance

Growing friendships

Having someone to love

an **I**nside job, go within

a **J**ourney of the heart

Knowing when to let go

Learning from your
mistakes

Making the best of
any situation

Not taking things
personally

Optional, so is misery

Progress not perfection

the **Q**uality of your
thoughts

Reverence for body,
mind and spirit

Spending time with
loved ones

Today well lived

Unconditional, no if's
and's or but's

Valuing feelings and needs

Whatever makes your
heart sing

Xpressing your truth
lovingly

Your choice, if not now,
when?

Zzzzzzz's,
a good night's sleep

© Meiji Stewart

The journey begins with the first step

How do you know when you've hit bottom? When you stop digging!

I would love to, but I need to talk to my sponsor first.

This is a suggested program and a judge suggested that I come.

You can't keep it unless you give it away.

When I'm feeling lousy it's never about what I have done. It's usually about what I haven't done.

People in recovery can be very opinionated and often wrong, but never in doubt.

Repression causes depression.

5

If you're looking for an easier, softer way, there are no directions.

My husband ran off with my sponsor – I miss her.

The original name for the Big Book was going to be "The Way Out."

How's the committee?
(Has it come to a meeting of the mind recently?)

The problem is alcoho<u>lis</u>m, not alcohol<u>was</u>ism.

H.O.W. – Honesty, Openmindedness, Willingness

When everything else fails, working with another will save the day.

If you want to change who you are, change what you do.

Overheard in a meeting: "Our leaders are but twisted servants."

The twelve steps are like wrenches in a toolbox – they'll fit any nut that walks in the door.

If you could take a pill that would make you a social drinker would you do it? Remember all it entitles you to is to have no more than 2 drinks. In fact you don't even drink 2 drinks – you have to walk out saying I'm feeling woozy.

If you make yourself available, you'll get what you need when you need it.

Warning: Carrying a grudge can be hazardous to your health.

All my life I wanted to be someone;
now I wish I had been more specific.

N.U.T.S. – Not Using The Steps

Alcoholics and addicts – fast talkers, slow
thinkers.

The Big Book is like a cookbook – you can read
it all day long and starve. You have to take the
action.

Life happens; joy is optional

You are heading towards a slip when you remember the good times more than the bad.

H.O.P.E. – Happy Our Program Exists

When you turn it over and don't let go of it, you will be upside down.

Keep your recovery first to make it last.

Do not give up. It is often the last key of the bunch that opens the door.

If I had known that I was going to live this long, I would have taken better care of myself.

Success means getting your "but" out of the way.

We together can do what I alone cannot.

The dry drunk's 8th step: make a list of all the people we have harmed and ask God to remove them.

Uncover, discover, discard.

Regrets aren't just about what we did, but a lot about what we didn't do.

When all else fails follow directions.

You aren't responsible for anyone's happiness but your own.

The truth will set you free but first it may piss you off.

There are no strangers in recovery – just friends we have never met.

**Don't quit 5 minutes before
the miracle happens.**

The first step in overcoming mistakes is to admit to them.

The best way to multiply happiness is to divide it.

Try the program for 90 days. If not satisfied we will be glad to refund your misery.

How old would you be if you didn't know how old you were?

Courage is fear that has said its prayers.

When you get to the end of your rope, tie a knot and hang on.

If you are waiting for your ship to come in – you may have already missed the boat.

Moving fast is not necessarily the same thing as going somewhere.

Poor me. Poor me. Pour me another drink.

Please Lord, teach us to laugh again, but,
God, don't let us ever forget that we cried.

Drop the rock.

Faith is our greatest gift. Sharing it with others
is our greatest responsibility.

I sought my soul, my soul I could not see; I sought my God – but he eluded me; I sought my brother, and found all three.

The only thing we can take with us when we leave this world is what we gave away.

Kind words cost so little but they mean so much.

This too shall pass.

I would rather see a sermon than hear one.

S.P.O.N.S.O.R. – Sober Person Offering Newcomers Suggestions On Recovery

If you stay humble, you will not stumble.

The biggest problem in the world could have been easily solved when it was small.

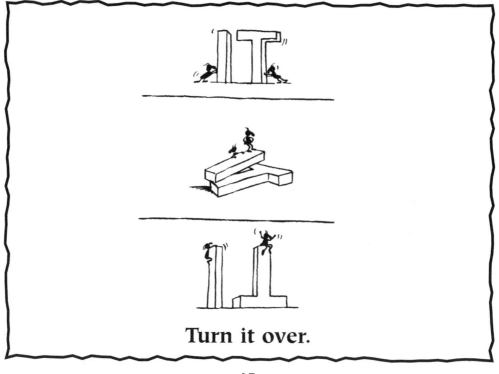

Turn it over.

G.O.D. – Good Orderly Direction

Came; came to; came to believe.

I am not responsible for your feelings-just my behavior. What you think of me is not my business.

It is not your job to point out other people's faults.

Who resigned and made you general manager of the universe?

Carry the message.

Pain instructs or it leads to more pain.

Wherever you go, there you are.

Don't be afraid to try something for fear you will fail; if you have not the will to try you have already failed.

Our neighbor's window looks much cleaner if we first wash our own.

To belittle is to be little.

The best way to find friends is to be one.

Time-for-a-meeting clue #72:
Feeling under the weather.

There is a big difference between "saying what you do" and "doing what you say."

Learn to listen; listen to learn.

Many of us fail to recognize "opportunity" because most of the time it is disguised as hard work.

Together—we can do it

Some people grumble because the roses have thorns instead of being grateful that the thorns have roses.

We must learn from the mistakes of others because we won't live long enough to make them all ourselves.

Don't look down on another person unless you are leaning over to help them up.

"You're just not serious about your program."

Recovery is a journey, not a destination. May your journey be long.

Yesterday is gone; forget it. Tomorrow never comes; don't worry. Today is here; get busy.

Willpower: our willingness to use a higher power.

The program is education without graduation.

Faith is not belief without proof, but trust without reservation.

People start slipping when they take other people's inventory instead of their own.

Change is a process, not an event.

Don't wait for your ship to come in – swim out and meet it.

When looking for faults use a mirror, not a telescope.

God can't give you anything new until you let go of the old.

Remember, we were all born to be happy, joyous and free.

Time for a meeting.

Sponsor saying #86: Who's not doing it your way today?

What a different world this would be if people would magnify their blessings the way they do their troubles.

The largest room in the world is the room for improvement.

To thine own self be true.

Imagination is a preview of life's coming attractions.

Thou shalt not *should* thyself.

Happiness is not a place to travel to. It's the journey of living life on life's terms.

The main purpose of this book is to help you find a power greater than yourself.

Maybe some of the people who go to meetings are well-adjusted, rational, mature adults – probably the Alateens.

Because my mind thinks something – doesn't necessarily make it so.

Sometimes I think my mind honestly believes it can kill me and get away with it.

Time wasted in getting even can never be used in getting ahead.

If you can't get what you want, learn to want what you get.

People who fly into rage always make a bad landing.

45

A mistake is evidence that someone has tried to do something.

I was the type of person who would eat and drink everything you had in your medicine cabinet.

I never got drunk watching another drink. I never got serenity watching others do the steps. This is a program of action.

D.E.N.I.A.L. – Don't Even Notice I Am Lying

There are no victims, only volunteers.

There is only one thing worse for an addict or alcoholic than bad fortune – good fortune.

If you don't drink again or use again, you don't ever have to go back to where you came from.

Do not disturb.
The Committee is in session.

There is absolutely no pain in change or growth. The pain is in the resistance to the change or growth.

The single most important thing to living life sober is a term called showing up.

What's the difference between a codependent and a pit bull? The pit bull usually knows when to let go.

If you are one of those people who has left undone the things that ought to have been done, and done the things that should not have been done, then you are in the right place.

A.S.K. – Ass-Saving Kit

Worry is a prayer for something you don't want.

Quit thinking. (It's what got you here.)

Thank God for all the drinks and drugs I've ever had, because it took them all to get me here.

Surrender is victory. We win by giving up the fight.

Heaven is just a new pair of glasses.

Recovery is an inside job.

Our problem is not information or insight, it is lack of action.

Pain is part of the program while suffering is optional.

If you are not grateful for your sobriety, you will not stay sober.

How come you are always running around looking for God? He isn't lost.

I came to this program to save my ass and found it was attached to my soul.

In recovery my drug of choice is anxiety.

If you take right actions, you'll get right results.

The only way to get to be right is to give up being right.

Failure is a necessary pathway to success.

There is no right or wrong – just consequences.

One drink or drug is too many and a thousand is not enough.

God gives us faces; we create our own expressions.

The difference between feeling grateful and being grateful is action.

Every year my sponsor sends me a get well card.

I used to be a hopeless dope fiend and I am now a dopeless hope fiend.

God's will for us is our well being.

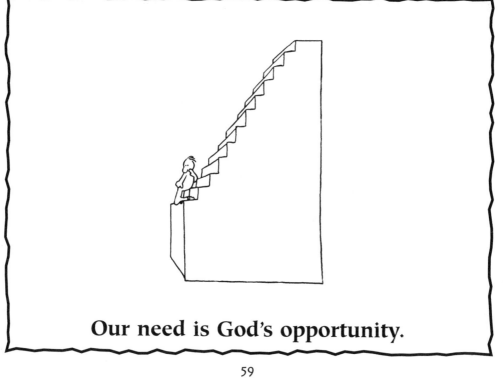

Our need is God's opportunity.

Forgiveness is not an event – it's a process.

Wake up, suit up, show up.

If I'm OK with me I have no need to make you wrong.

You can't do it for me but I can't do it for myself.

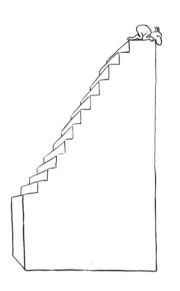

I can't handle it God – You take over.

I used to drink and drug to make other people more interesting.

Yesterday is a canceled check, tomorrow is a promissory note, today is cash in hand, spend it wisely.

E.G.O. – Edging God Out

OUT OF TOWN

**Geographic: leaving town
with one's ass on fire.**

You can be about as happy as you decide to be.

The journey of a thousand miles begins with the first step.

What you resist persists.

If you don't want to get hit by a train, don't hang out at the tracks.

I was a periodic drinker – I drank period.

When you look in the mirror, you are looking at the problem, but, remember, you are also looking at the solution.

If your life worked so well, what are you doing here?

Some things have to be believed to be seen.

There is an answer to everything – it's just a matter of finding it.

I worry all the time about being obsessive compulsive.

Happiness is a by-product of right living.

We are all here because we aren't all there.

Happiness is opening the refrigerator door and seeing your sponsor's face on the side of a milk carton.

Making an amends is like taking an inside shower.

Be who you are, where you're at, when you're there.

Don't fear taking a big step when one is needed.
You can't cross a chasm in two small jumps.

When you make a 12-step call and you don't drink, it is successful.

B.I.G. B.O.O.K. – Believing In God Beats Our Old Knowledge

I am not overdrawn, just underdeposited.

When they are ready, you can do no wrong. If they are not ready, you can do no right.

Suicide – a permanent solution to a temporary problem.

Any chance I had of being the victim I took because it was a lot easier to blame you than to look at my own life.

I am not a human being having a spiritual experience, I am a spiritual being having a human experience.

Using gave me the feeling of a job well done without having done a thing.

Self-esteem comes from doing esteemable acts.

The Twelve Steps gives us the tools that allow us to be exactly who we want to be.

We don't drink or use, no matter what.

73

I came from a normal family, both my parents are dysfunctional.

If you change your action, your attitude will change.

I am an all-or-nothing kind of person. The only thing I've done in moderation is the steps.

I'm not one of those people who has memorized the Big Book – I figure that's OK because it's all written down for me to look up.

It's the twelve steps, not the twelve standstills.

We all know that God never closes one door without opening another... but it can be painful in the hallway.

PORCELAIN ALTAR   NAPPING

MEDITATING   ISOMETRICS

Remember the good old days?

I am a seeker of external solutions to internal problems.

Survived hell – found heaven.

Intimacy... "into me you see."

God says "no" a lot but all he is really saying is wait – there is something better for you down the road.

The voices in my head often shout to me as I'm about to start sharing at a meeting. "Dramatize it! Dramatize it!"

S.L.I.P. – Sobriety Losing Its Priority

People have the right to not recover.

Few alcoholics or addicts blame themselves before exhausting all other possibilities.

I didn't know I was the problem and that wherever I went I took me with me.

I don't have to like a situation, but it is important that I like myself in it.

If you don't like the warts, let go of the frog.

There are some days when I say: "What program?" "God who?"

God please remind me that nothing is going to
happen to me that you and I can't handle.

Sitting in meetings doesn't make you a member anymore than sitting in a chicken coop makes you a chicken.

Problems have a high infant mortality rate.

I wanted to be famous and God made me anonymous.

**Time-for-a-meeting clue #128:
Feeling that you're "going insane."**

If you are hating somebody, you might as well call them up in the middle of the night because they are sleeping like a log while you are the one losing sleep!

Nothing is as sweet as the smell of hope in the air.

I love information, stacking it, filing it, alphabetizing it, sorting it and reviewing it over and over again and even sharing it with you – in fact I love everything about information except using it.

If you drink near beer, consider yourself near drunk, and then consider yourself near sober.

Meeting makers make it.

No matter where you've been or what you have done, somebody has "been there" or "done that" before you.

I thought I had it all together when I got here, but together we have it all.

Remember, God still makes house calls.

I tried to think my way out of lots of problems. It never worked once.

Poverty never stops an alcoholic or addict from drinking or using. It may stop them from buying shoes for the kids, but it won't stop their habit.

If you wait until you're not scared you'll never do anything. This program taught me to work with fear.

Reason to be grateful #1,034: No more rugburns caused by the repeated need to pray (beg & grovel) for forgiveness either to God, to one's spouse, family or friends.

Everybody is my teacher. Some teach me what to do; some teach me what not to do.

God works through people and he gets twice the result for the same amount of work – for both are helped.

The longer you've been in recovery, the more successful you've been in the past.

If it ain't broke, don't fix it.

If you don't like the effect, don't produce the cause.

Recovery is not a destination, but a road we travel.

All the answers to all of our problems are contained in the sharing in the meetings.

God does for me what I can't do for myself.

Forgiveness is very important. It's not the people that I'm busy hating that are suffering – it's usually the people around me who take the punishment.

God can't give you anything new until you let go of the old.

A.C.T.I.O.N. – Any Change To Improve Our Nature

You cannot be rejected by another human being – all they can tell you is what their limits are.

There's room for more than one opinion and none of them has to be wrong.

When there's a chip on your shoulder, it indicates that there's wood nearby.

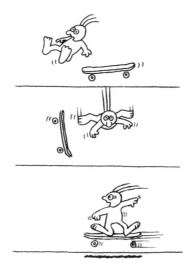

Progress not perfection.

My drug of choice was whatever you had.

I went to 8 years of Catholic school. I majored in guilt and minored in shame.

Depression: when you're taking more than you're giving.

God grant me the courage to change the things I cannot accept.

Think God. Thank God.

If you don't sit up front, you may go out the back and use.

I have learned that when amends are made to me – I say 'thank you' but I don't have to go back for seconds.

My spouse had a drinking problem. It was me.

Thinking about what you'll say before you share, or what you should have said after you share means you missed the meeting.

Having a relationship in early recovery is like pouring Miracle Grow on your character defects.

I'm still acting the way I want to be, so that one day I will be the way I act.

Mixed emotions is what you get watching your child go down the aisle with someone whose 5th step you've heard.

It took me a long time to realize that when I hate somebody it doesn't hurt them. Only me.

P.R.O.G.R.A.M. – People Relying On God Relaying A Message

Helping hands are God's hands.

Friends Are...

Amazing, cherish them.

Blessings, acknowledge them.

Caring, allow them.

Dependable, rely on them.

Encouraging, hear them.

Fallible, love them.

Gifts, unwrap them.

Healing, be with them.

Important, value them.

Juicy, savor them.

Kind, delight in them.

Loyal, mirror them.

Magical, soar with them.

Necessary, cultivate them.

Optimistic, support them.

Priceless, treasure them.

Quirky, enjoy them.

Rare, hold on to them.

Strong, lean on them.

Teachers, learn from them.

Understanding, talk to them.

Vulnerable, embrace them.

Warmhearted, listen to them.

Xtraordinary, recognize them.

Young at heart, play with them.

Zany, laugh with them.

© Meiji Stewart

102

Life is a dance when you do the steps.

103

The program is for participants, not spectators.

Having a tremendous capacity for alcohol may make us proud, but it's like telling someone who has tuberculosis that they cough very well.

When does it get better? It gets better when your behavior changes.

A 12-step meeting is God's workshop.

Be careful of your thoughts; they may become words at any moment.

Our faith should be our steering wheel not our spare tire.

A winner makes commitments; a loser makes promises.

God never asks about our ability or our inability, just our availability.

H.A.L.T. (Don't get too) Hungry, Angry, Lonely, Tired

Remember, the mightiest oak was once a little nut that held its ground.

It says: "here are the steps we *took*," not *suggested*, not *understood*.

I still take people's inventories. I just don't announce them at group level.

Winners – people who tell you what they did and not people who tell you what they think you ought to do.

Believe in your magic.

You are the problem, but you are also the solution.

Reason to be grateful #863: you learn to wake up instead of coming to.

Improve your memory; tell the truth.

Numb is dumb; feel to heal.

**Know God; know peace.
No God; no peace.**

Comfort the disturbed and disturb the comfortable.

If you say "don't" – I want to.

I can have faith in the things I have not seen because of the things I have seen.

Let us love you until you can love yourself.

Today is the tomorrow you worried about yesterday.

For peace of mind, resign as general manager of the universe.

People will be more impressed by the depth of your conviction than the height of your logic.

I've suffered a great many catastrophes in my life. Most of them never happened.

What a big difference there is between giving advice and lending a hand.

Guilt is concerned with the past. Worry is concerned about the future. Contentment enjoys the present.

If you want to make an easy job seem mighty hard, just keep putting it off.

What you are speaks so loudly that I can't hear a word you are saying.

Welcome to recovery – the largest group of people in the world to go from adolescence to senility without passing through maturity.

I'd climb a tree to tell a lie when I could have just as easily stayed on the ground and told the truth.

Sometimes you might want to share your "brilliant idea" with friends before you take action. Remember, your best thinking got you here in the first place.

F.E.A.R. – Face Everything And Recover

Reality is whatever it is, the way it is.

I know that God knows what's best for me because I am living a life I never wanted any part of, I'm a person I never would have wanted to know and I'm happier than I've ever been.

**Shared joy is double joy;
shared sorrow is half sorrow.**

Most people wish to serve God – but only in an advisory capacity.

Be more concerned with what God thinks about you than what people think about you.

God plus one is always a majority.

We make a living by what we get. We make a life by what we give.

S.T.E.P.S. – Solutions To Every Problem Sober

The difference between ordinary and extraordinary is that little extra.

To forgive is to set a prisoner free and to discover that the prisoner was you.

To be upset over what you don't have is to waste what you do have.

The expression of surrender is to live your life in harmony with the universe.

Our need is God's opportunity.

Sponsors: have one, use one, be one.

If you find a path with no obstacles, it probably doesn't lead anywhere.

First we work the program because we have to. Then we work the program because we are willing to. Finally we work the program because we want to.

When you do all the talking you only learn what you already know.

Fear is the darkroom where negatives are developed.

Let go, let God.

Formula for failure: trying to please everyone.

Before I came to the program I had no choice. I had to use. Now I have a choice.

The elevator is broken; use the steps.

You are exactly where God wants you to be.

There is nothing so bad that getting high can't make it worse.

You are only as sick as your secrets.

I surrender. Where is the meeting?

Please do not feel personally, irrevocably, totally responsible for everything. That's my job. Love, God.

You can't go back and have a brand new start, but anybody can start now and have a brand new end.

When God measures us, He puts the tape around the heart instead of the head.

Be careful about the bridges you burn, because one might turn out to be the one you later want to cross.

Call your sponsor before, not after, you take your first drink.

Nothing is so bad that relapse won't make it worse.

I can't handle it, God. You take over.

A problem shared is a problem halved.

"The Family"

Trust God, clean house, help others.

Insanity is repeating the same mistake over and over again and expecting different results.

There is no chemical solution to a spiritual problem.

Bring the body and the mind will follow.

Time-for-a-meeting-clue #38: The feeling of having a lot on your mind.

F.I.N.E. – (I'm) Frustrated, Insecure, Neurotic, Emotional

Get to know a stranger, do a 4th step today.

Thank you God for all you have given me, for all you have taken away from me, and for all you have left me.

Let nothing disturb you. Let nothing frighten you. Everything passes away except God.

The best way out is almost always through.

Courage is a state of mind that enables me to face whatever I have to face without having to drink or use.

K.I.S.S. – Keep It Simple, Sweetheart

Failure isn't falling down, it's not getting back up.

Big Book suggestion: read the black parts.

It's a program of attraction, not promotion.

It says in the Big Book: *"We insist on being happy."*

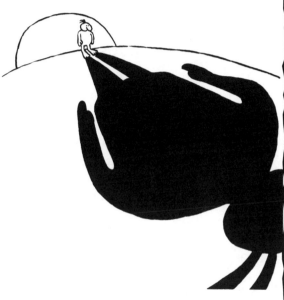

Worry gives a small thing a big shadow.

As long as we work the steps and don't drink or use – our lives change and we stay clean and serene.

We are not in recovery to change the world. We are in recovery to learn how to function within the world.

The most important relationship is between God and me.

Build bridges, not walls.

Practice love and service at work and at home and not just in meetings.

We don't make amends for approval or forgiveness. We make amends to clean up our side of the street and to stay sober.

You cannot think your way into right actions. You have to act your way into right thinking.

Go for it.

The road to success is always under construction.

Long to live in order to live long.

Everything I ever let go of had claw marks all over it.

If you are not happy today, what day are you waiting for?

God loves you and I am trying.

The only thing you can control in your life is your attitude.

I've stopped drinking and using, but not pissing people off.

Of all the things I've lost, I miss my mind the most.

The back half of the room at meetings is known as the denial section.

Getting stuck means you are in between surrenders.

It's not what leads you to drinking, it's where the drinking lead you.

145

You loved me when I could not love myself. You taught me how to love you and for that I am extremely grateful.

People in recovery are creatures that, told "thou shalt not", have no choice but to do it.

There's one thing that I've never been addicted to and that's work.

Paranoia Anonymous

Worry is interest on fear.

It takes one month of sobriety for every year of drinking and using just to get our brains out of hock.

Nothing succeeds like persistence.

I don't know what is enough, until I find out what is more than enough.

If you want to feel better, clean house. If you want to get better, find God.

We usually condemn in others what we dislike in ourselves.

Alcohol and drugs are solvents; they will remove everything from your life.

You go to enough meetings and eventually you'll meet someone and go on a date. You get taken to a meeting then afterwards you go out for coffee and talk about the meeting. At the end of the first date it can be confusing, though, because you're not sure if you should kiss or say the Lord's Prayer.

Take what you can use and leave the rest.

When I was a kid safe sex meant locking the car door.

My sponsor told me they don't lock you up for being crazy, only for acting crazy.

It's the things I do wrong, my failings, that are often the bridge to other people.

Hazelden Foundation, a national nonprofit organization founded in 1949, helps people reclaim their lives from the disease of addiction. Built on decades of knowledge and experience, Hazelden's comprehensive approach to addiction addresses the full range of individual, family, and professional needs, including addiction treatment and continuing care services for youth and adults, publishing, research, higher learning, public education, and advocacy.

A life of recovery is lived "one day at a time." Hazelden publications, both educational and inspirational, support and strengthen lifelong recovery. In 1954, Hazelden published *Twenty-Four Hours a Day,* the first daily meditation book for recovering alcoholics, and Hazelden continues to publish works to inspire and guide individuals in treatment and recovery, and their loved ones. Professionals who work to prevent and treat addiction also turn to Hazelden for evidence-based curricula, informational materials, and videos for use in schools, treatment programs, and correctional programs.

Through published works, Hazelden extends the reach of hope, encouragement, help, and support to individuals, families, and communities affected by addiction and related issues.

For questions about Hazelden publications,
please call **800-328-9000** or visit us online at **hazelden.org/bookstore.**

About the Author

Meiji Stewart has created other gift books, designs, and writings that may be of interest to you. Please visit www.puddledancer.com or call 1-877-EMPATHY (367-2849) for more information about any of the items listed below.

(1) **Keep Coming Back** - Over two hundred gift products including greeting cards, wallet cards, bookmarks, magnets, bumper stickers, gift books, and more. (Free catalog available from Hazelden at 800-328-9000.)

(2) **ABC Writings** - Titles include *Children Are, Children Need, Creativity Is, Dare To, Fathers Are, Friends Are, Grandparents, Great Teachers, Happiness Is, I Am, Life Is, Loving Families, May You Always Have, Mothers Are, Recovery Is, Soulmates, Success Is,* and many more works in progress. Many of these ABC writings are available as posters (from Portal Publications) at your favorite poster and gift store, or directly from Hazelden on a variety of gift products.

(3) **Nonviolent Communication: A Language of Compassion** by Marshall Rosenberg. (from PuddleDancer Press) - Jack Canfield (*Chicken Soup for the Soul* author) says, "I believe the principles and techniques in this book can literally change the world – but more importantly, they can change the quality of your life with your spouse, your children, your neighbors, your co-workers, and everyone else you interact with. I cannot recommend it highly enough." Available from Hazelden and your local and on-line bookstores. For more information about The Center for Nonviolent Communication please visit www.cnvc.org.